# ROCK CLIMBING

## The Fundamentals

**John R. Kascenska II**
**Horace T. Bone**
*North Carolina State University*

**KENDALL/HUNT PUBLISHING COMPANY**
2460 Kerper Boulevard P.O. Box 539 Dubuque, Iowa 52004-0539

Cover photo by Horace Bone, Mt. Kenya.

Printed in the United States of America
10  9  8  7  6  5  4  3  2  1

# CONTENTS

Preface **v**

Acknowledgements **v**

Chapter I   **An Introduction to Rock Climbing 1**

Chapter II   **Basic Equipment 5**

Chapter III   **Knots, Runners, And Harnesses 13**

Chapter IV   **Movement on Rock 19**

Chapter V   **Belaying 25**

Chapter VI   **Placement of Protection 33**

Chapter VII   **Rappelling/Ascending 39**

Chapter VIII   **Climbing Ratings 49**

Chapter IX   **Ethics for Climbing and the Environment 51**

References **54**

Glossary **55**

# PREFACE

**Rock Climbing: The Fundamentals** is written to introduce basic rock climbing skills, yet also serve as a resource for climbers who wish to further enhance their skills. Safety is an underlying theme of each chapter.

The first chapter introduces the beginner to rock climbing activities. Chapter Two introduces basic rock climbing equipment, while Chapter Three discusses and illustrates knots. The various climbing techniques are described and illustrated in Chapter Four.

In addition, Chapters Five through Seven include the rock climbing skills of belaying, the use of natural and artificial anchors, and the techniques of rappelling and ascending.

Chapter Eight describes common rating systems. Finally, this book addresses ethics of particular interest to climbers.

It is our sincere desire that this text serve as a guide for beginners to gain sound knowledge and skill in rock climbing. In no way, however, should this book be viewed as a substitute for experience and/or professional instruction. In addition, it is our goal that **Rock Climbing: The Fundamentals** serve as a teaching aid for those professionals who instruct basic rock climbing courses in schools, colleges, and universities.

John R. Kascenska II
Horace T. Bone

# ACKNOWLEDGEMENTS

The authors would like to thank those individuals who contributed to the completion of this book. Aram Attarian's review of the content and accuracy of the text is greatly appreciated. The authors would also like to thank Kay Summerlin for her contributions in regard to the illustrations of climbing technique and Beth Kascenska for her contributions in regard to the photography, grammatical review, and illustrations of knots.

# AN INTRODUCTION TO ROCK CLIMBING

I

## The Sport of Rock Climbing

Participation in outdoor pursuits has become an increasingly popular recreational activity. Although considered a segment of the more broad pursuit of mountaineering (or mountain climbing), rock climbing has in recent years begun to develop into a sport of its own. Rock climbing is the activity of ascending boulders or cliffs. Like other outdoor pursuits, rock climbing has experienced tremendous growth. Rock climbing, for many years, has been a favorite activity among organizations such as outing clubs and is taught by professional outdoor adventure organizations such as Outward Bound, The National Outdoor Leadership School, and other private outdoor programs and guide services. Rock climbing has, in several instances, become a segment of the formal educational system, as increasing numbers of colleges, universities and private schools now teach rock climbing. In addition, rock climbing has become a part of an increasing number of municipal recreation programs.

Although every outdoor recreational activity presents its own degree of excitement, none can offer the same feeling as that derived from rock climbing. Those participating in rock climbing may be seeking individual challenge, a sense of adventure, or an opportunity to enjoy the outdoors. Even if it is just climbing a tree in the backyard, most people have participated in some type of climbing activity. Although some individuals may develop a fear of heights, many become fascinated with high places, graduating from climbing trees in the backyard to scaling boulders, rock cliffs and high peaks.

Rock climbing is also an activity that can be enjoyed by those of a wide range of ages and abilities. Many individuals, however, arrive ill-prepared with little or no knowledge and experience to safely ascend even the easiest of climbs. A safe rock climbing experience requires the use of proper equipment as well as the exercise of good judgment. In many instances, the responsibility for a safe climbing experience is placed solely upon equipment. Although the climber must rely upon equipment to a certain degree, safe acts must come from the climber. Climbers must be well aware of their abilities and limitations as well as the performance of the equipment. A famous mountaineer once stated that, "Today's climber . . . carries his courage in his rucksack . . . Faith in equipment has replaced faith in oneself" (Wilson, 1980). In other words, climbers must develop good judgment. Judgment is the ability to make sound decisions based upon knowledge *and* experience. Not every climbing situation is the same. Climbers must be able to analyze a climbing problem, make sound decisions, and apply their skills to solve the problem at hand.

1

Although no text should function as a substitute for experience, *Rock Climbing*: *The Fundamentals* can serve as a guide to introduce the beginner to the basic skills. It is the intent of the authors that skills learned through this text *and* practiced in actual climbing situations will enhance one's competencies, while improving one's abilities to make good climbing decisions. In addition, experienced climbers may wish to utilize the text as a vehicle to introduce others to the activity. Rock climbing is by nature a dangerous activity, so it is doubly important that beginning climbers have a complete understanding of the essential skills.

## Types of Climbing

A description of the different types of climbing is provided below. Although a specialized branch of mountaineering, rock climbing can assume different forms. These include bouldering, top-roped climbing, lead climbing, aid climbing, and solo climbing.

Bouldering is the traverse or ascent of a route a few feet off the ground, without using a rope for protection. Bouldering is a good activity for all climbers to improve climbing technique. Although the consequences of a fall from a few feet are minimal, spotters should be used, especially where a climber could be injured from exposed roots or rocks. A spotter is an individual who follows the climber as he ascends or traverses the rock. Should the climber fall, it is the responsibility of the spotter to break the climber's fall while protecting the head and back areas. Proper spotting technique includes holding the hands high with palms facing outward and placing one foot in front of the other to provide a more stable base of support (Fig. 1.1). Helmets are advised for both the climber and spotter.

**Figure 1.1** A climber with a spotter demonstrating proper spotting technique.

Top-roped climbing is an activity in which the climber is protected by a rope that is anchored from above (Fig. 1.2). The climber is tied to one end of the rope, while a second person serves as the belayer and anchors the other end. Should the climber fall, the belayer managing the rope is able to protect the climber by anchoring the rope using one of a variety of belay methods. The rope is only used as a means of safeguarding the route and not as a means for ascending. Specific methods for belaying are discussed in Chapter V.

Lead climbing is an activity in which the climber, with a rope attached to the harness, climbs a route periodically placing intermediate anchors as he ascends (Fig. 1.3). In the event of a fall, the climber will be stopped by the intermediate anchors. The higher the in-

Figure 1.3 Lead climbing.

Figure 1.2 A climber on a top-roped climb.

dividual climbs above the last piece of protection, the greater the distance he may fall. It is easy to see why lead climbing has been referred to as "climbing on the sharp end of the rope."

Aid climbing is considered a part of lead climbing in which the climber ascends a route by using ropes and hardware to bear his weight. Belayers who follow the lead climber may also aid the route.

Solo climbing is the activity of climbing routes without a rope for protection. Climbers who participate in this type of climbing usually have many years of experience. They are also well aware of their abilities and limitations. It is not recommended that climbers participate in this type of climbing, as the consequences of a fall are usually fatal.

Now that a picture has been painted as to what is involved in the many varieties of rock climbing, the process for learning the basic skills can begin. The order of chapters that follow will allow the beginning climber to learn fundamental rock climbing skills in a sensible progression. Basic equipment will be discussed next, followed by knots, movement on rock, belaying, placement of protection, rappelling and ascending, climbing ratings, and finally, ethics for climbing and the environment. A glossary of terms can be found in the appendix.

—John R. Kascenska, II—

# BASIC EQUIPMENT

II

## Introduction

This chapter introduces the beginning rock climber to the most basic equipment, but also describes the latest and most effective types of equipment. Although new innovations in equipment continuously evolve, the basic gear has remained almost unchanged. This includes ropes and webbing, harnesses, carabiners, helmets, clothing and footwear.

## Climbing Rope

Ropes used in the infancy of rock climbing and mountaineering were made of natural fibers (manila, flax, hemp, sisal, and cotton) woven into three strands. Ropes manufactured with this three-strand type of construction are referred to as *laid* ropes (Fig. 2.1). These natural fiber ropes were also much shorter than ropes used in modern climbing. According to Wheelock (1982), the lead climber would in many cases ascend a section of the planned route while those following might climb the rope or be bodily hauled to the top of the completed route. Natural fiber ropes had some distinct disadvantages in that they tended to absorb moisture and deteriorated over a relatively short period of time. This weakened the rope significantly, and the natural fiber ropes would not likely have held the climber's weight in a severe fall.

**Figure 2.1** Examples of laid rope (on left) and kernmantel rope (on right).

Today's climbing ropes, however, are far superior to their predecessors. With the formation of the U. S. Mountain Troops in the 1940's, an investigation was initiated to select the best possible rope for military use. It was determined that nylon was the superior rope material, providing advantages in terms of strength, aging characteristics, and elasticity. These nylon ropes were of a laid construction and soon became available for civilian use.

Although climbing ropes of laid construction are still manufactured, most climbers use a rope with a nylon core under a braided sheath. Ropes of this type of construction are referred to as *kernmantel* ropes (Fig. 2.1). Eleven millimeters is the popular diameter for kernmantel rope with standard lengths of either 45 or 50 meters.

Climbing ropes are viewed by climbers as their lifeline; their most important piece of equipment. Although fairly strong and resistant to mildew, aging, and some chemicals, modern climbing ropes need special care. First, the climber should be careful to not step on the rope. This practice may severely damage the rope by imbedding grains of dirt and sand, thus adding to the wear and tear of the nylon fibers. Second, allowing the rope to run across sharp edges will cut rope fibers and may cause rope failure. Third, when the climbing rope is stored, it needs to be coiled and placed in a dry, cool environment. Fourth, prolonged exposure to ultraviolet rays and contact with petroleum and some chemical products will cause a weakening of the rope fibers. Finally, climbing ropes that become excessively dirty may be washed in luke warm water with a mild detergent. They should be rinsed well and hung to air dry.

Two methods for coiling a climbing rope may be used. The classic method for coiling a rope is to make a series of ovals with the rope. The finished coil should then be secured as shown in figure 2.2a–d. A second method for coiling the rope is the lap coil. While holding both ends of the rope in one hand, take two arm spans of rope (Fig. 2.3a). The remaining rope is then "lapped" from one side of the hand to the other (Fig. 2.3b). When all rope has been lapped, the coil is then secured with the initial two arm spans (Fig. 2.3c–d). The lap coiling technique is most effective for reducing the kinking that tends to occur as a result of employing the classic coil.

Even with proper use and care, climbing ropes will not last forever. It is a good practice to inspect the climbing rope before each use for signs of excessive wear. This can be done by both visual inspection and feel. Laid ropes are easier to inspect because most of the rope fibers are quite visible. Cuts and/or heavy abrasions can be easily seen. In contrast, kernmantel ropes are more difficult to inspect because the protective sheath does not allow internal damage to be seen. However, a kernmantel rope should be considered suspect if any unusual lumps, indentations or hard spots are felt. Cuts or severe abrasions through the sheath are also suspect. Seriously damaged areas near the end of a rope can be cut off, while the remainder can still be used. As a rough guide, a climbing rope that receives moderate weekend use (top-roped climbing) may last a period of two years, but this depends greatly upon how the rope has been treated. Ropes used more frequently may need to be replaced each year or earlier. Manufacturers suggest that ropes subjected to one hard lead fall should be retired. Keeping a written log of rope use will help in making the decision of when to retire the rope. The bottom line is not to wait too long!

## Webbing

The development of tubular nylon webbing in widths of 1–2 in. is useful in the construction of slings and harnesses (see Chapter III). Webbing should also be inspected frequently for signs of heavy fraying and discarded if found to be cut, heavily abraded, or showing signs of hardening. Many climbers replace webbing at the end of the climbing season.

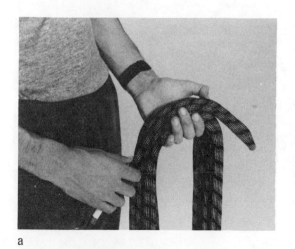

a

b

c

d

**Figure 2.2a-d** The classic method for coiling a rope.

## Harnesses

The climbing harness (or sit harness) is a web-like belt system worn by a climber to which a climbing rope is attached. Climbing harnesses may be constructed from a length of 1–2 in. webbing. Although manufactured harnesses are common, constructing a harness from 1–2 in. webbing is a skill that all climbers

should learn. One method for constructing a harness is included at the end of Chapter III.

Expensive manufactured harnesses are as safe and usually more comfortable than tied harnesses. Manufactured harnesses are either of a one or two-piece construction. The one-piece harness is usually constructed with a two-inch waist band and connecting leg loops. The two-piece harness usually consists of a

a

b

c

d

**Figure 2.3a-d** The lap method for coiling a rope.

padded waist belt (sometimes referred to as a swami) with detachable leg loops. Whichever type is used, there are several things to look for in a manufactured harness. First, it is important that the harness be the correct size. Most manufactured harnesses are sold by waist size. Second, the climber should be familiar with the manufacturer's directions to ensure proper use of the harness. If the harness is secured with a buckle, there should be enough of the webbing left over so it can be doubled back through the buckle (Fig. 2.4). The nylon webbing may slip back through the buckle if not doubled back. Finally, like climbing ropes, harnesses should be inspected before each use. Inspect all of the webbing for signs of abrasions or cuts. A climber should also check the stitching in the harness to be sure it is intact. Many harnesses will contain stitching that is a different color from the webbing to aid this inspection.

**Figure 2.4** A manufactured harness with the webbing doubled back through the buckle for safety.

Chest harnesses can be used in conjunction with the sit harness to help keep the climber in an upright position after a fall has occurred (Fig. 2.5). Chest harnesses are recommended for lead climbers. It is important to remember, however, that chest harnesses should *never* be used alone. There is too great a chance that the chest harness could slide up and over the head in the event of a fall.

## Helmets

Climbing helmets are designed with two specific purposes in mind. First, they are designed to protect the head from falling objects (rocks, carabiners, etc.), and secondly to protect the head in the event of a fall. Anyone who has studied the sport of rock climbing has probably observed that it has become common for climbers to not wear a climbing helmet. Some climbers claim that helmets are heavy, hot or tend to obstruct their field of vision. Manufacturers, however, have been truly mindful to construct helmets that allow greater field of vision and are lightweight and strong.

Two philosophies are prevalent regarding their use. One philosophy is that helmets

**Figure 2.5** A manufactured harness used in conjunction with a chest harness.

should only be worn when lead climbing or when climbing in an area where rockfall is an obvious threat. A second philosophy is that helmets should always be worn. It is recommended, however, that helmets be worn during *all* rock climbing activities. Even the assumed safeness of a top-roped climb can easily lead to a serious head injury, such as a scalp laceration, concussion or skull fracture. For example, an incident occurred in which a relatively inexperienced climber was attempting to scale a short, top-roped route. Halfway up the route, the climber traversed too far to the right, creating a dangerous pendulum situation. Subsequently, the climber fell, swung to the left and hit the back of his head against the cliff. Fortunately, the climber was wearing a helmet and only suffered a headache. Although an ob-

**Figure 2.6** Climbing helmets.

vious error in judgment had been made by the climber, errors in judgment can even be made by experienced climbers. In short, a helmet will provide adequate protection against head injury. Several models are shown in figure 2.6.

## Carabiners

Carabiners are oval, D-shaped or pear-shaped snaplinks that have a variety of uses (Fig. 2.7). All carabiners have spring-loaded gates that can be easily opened, but otherwise remain closed. Some models also have a locking thumb screw to prevent the gate from accidentally opening. In the early days of climbing, all carabiners were constructed of steel. Carabiners are still manufactured from steel, and these are usually utilized by rescue groups and climbing schools. The majority of carabiners, however, are constructed of aluminum alloys that make them lightweight as well as strong. Appropriate uses of carabiners will be discussed in further detail in Chapters V–VII.

## Clothing and Footwear

Beginning rock climbers will discover that clothing worn for climbing should be functional. Two guidelines should be followed: cloth-

**Figure 2.7** Non-locking (left top and bottom) and locking (right top and bottom) carabiners.

ing must be loose fitting to allow freedom of movement, and one should dress appropriately for the climate. This may include bringing along a set of lightweight raingear, pile jacket, hat, and gloves depending on the season.

Footwear is another important accessory for the climber. Although sneakers or hiking boots are often used by a climber on a first adventure, shoes designed for climbing will definitely improve one's feel for the rock and increase the chances of ascending difficult routes. A shoe designed for climbing closely resembles a tennis shoe with a smooth sticky rubber sole that allows the shoe to have maximal contact with the rock (Fig. 2.8). This rubber is also hard enough so that it will enable one to stand on tiny footholds. Climbing shoes should fit snugly to give a good "feel" for the rock, but should never fit so tightly that they cause pain.

## Climbing Protection

As described in Chapter I, climbers need to establish anchor points from which they can set up a top-rope or protect themselves when lead climbing. Climbers will, in most climbing situations, try to utilize some natural feature of

**Figure 2.8** A typical rock climbing shoe.

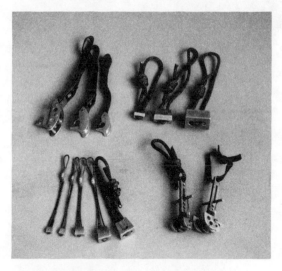

**Figure 2.9** Example of artificial climbing protection.

the cliff as an anchor. For example this natural feature may be a tree or horn of rock. When these natural features are not available, some artificial means of anchoring or "protection" will be needed. Protection used in place of natural anchors include chocks and mechanical devices in a variety of shapes and sizes (Fig. 2.9). Climbing protection is discussed in further detail in Chapter VII.

—John R. Kascenska, II—

# III

# KNOTS, RUNNERS, AND HARNESSES

Figure 3.1 The overhand knot.

## Knots

A knot has been described as "a con-figuration in ropes to join two lines together, or to fasten a rope into a loop or onto some other object (Wheelock, 1982)." Knots used in climbing were selected because they can be easily tied and trusted to hold, as long as they have been properly constructed. Knots used in climbing can also be easily recognized because they have a distinct shape or pattern. Although there are many knots that are used in climbing, the beginning climber can safely climb by using only a few. Useful knots are described and illustrated below. The construction of runners and climbing harnesses is also presented.

### Overhand Knot

The overhand is generally used as a back-up or "safety knot" to prevent other more complex knots from coming untied. It is easily constructed by making a loop and passing one end through the loop (Fig. 3.1).

### Figure-8 Follow-Through Knot

The figure-8 follow-through is commonly used to attach a rope to the climber's harness

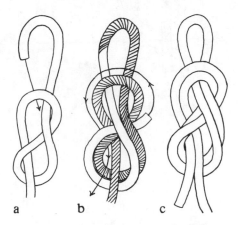

Figure 3.2a-c The figure--8 follow-through knot.

but can also be used to attach two ropes of equal diameter together. The figure-8 follow-through is also the safest and strongest knot for attaching a rope to the harness. At least 5–5 1/2 ft of rope is needed to tie this knot. It is constructed by making a loop, and then taking another turn with the end of the rope before it is passed through the loop (Fig. 3.2a). This first step creates the figure-8 shape that gives the knot its name. The end of the rope is passed through the harness and re-traces the figure-8 shape first constructed (Fig. 3.2b–c). An overhand knot tied directly above the figure-8 will prevent the end of the rope from slipping back through the loop.

### Figure-8 on a Bight

The figure-8 on a bight is tied by doubling the rope over, making a figure-eight shape as shown below and passing the bight through the

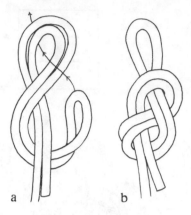

**Figure 3.3a-b** The figure-8 on a bight.

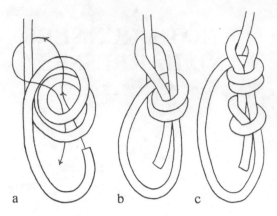

**Figure 3.5a-c** The double bowline.

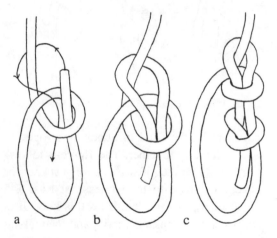

**Figure 3.4a-c** The bowline.

loop (Fig. 3.3). This knot is useful for constructing a non-slipping loop.

## Bowline

The bowline can be used to attach a climbing rope to a harness and can also be used to tie a rope around a climber's waist. If tied correctly, this knot will produce a non-slipping loop (Fig. 3.4a–c). The double bowline, a variation of the single bowline, is used by some climbers (Fig. 3.5), because it increases the strength of the knot by as much as five per-

cent. Both the single and double bowline should always be secured with an overhand.

## Water Knot

The water knot is used to tie two ends of webbing together. It is easily constructed by first tying an overhand, making sure to leave at least a 4–5 in. tail (Fig. 3.6a). This overhand is then re-traced with the other end (Fig. 3.6b). It is important to tighten this knot by pulling on the two tails and then on the two remaining ends. This knot should be checked periodically since it has a tendency to loosen.

## Double Fisherman's Knot

The double fisherman's knot is easily tied by modifying the overhand and will allow the climber to attach one end of rope to another of the same or dissimilar diameters. Two ends are first gathered in one of the climber's hands with each of the two ends running in opposite directions. With end #1, two loops (the second behind the first) are made around end #2 and passed through the backside of the loops (Fig. 3.7a). The same is done with end #2 around end #1 (Fig. 3.7b). The two knots are then pulled together (Fig. 3.7c). It should be noted

14

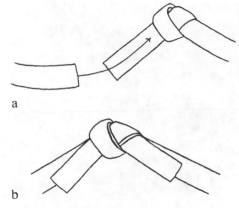

a

b

**Figure 3.6a-b**  The water knot.

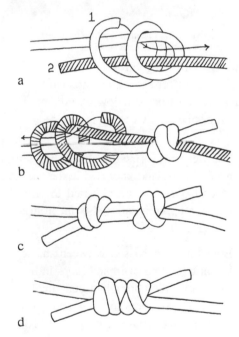

a

b

c

d

**Figure 3.7a-d**  The double fisherman's knot.

that the double fisherman's knot is difficult to untie when weight has been put on the knot.

## Square Knot

The square knot is generally not used in rock climbing, because when used alone it is not as effective as other knots. However, for

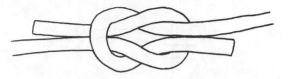

**Figure 3.8**  The square knot.

holding up the leg loops in the construction of a climbing harness from 1–2 in. tubular webbing, it is useful. The square knot is illustrated above (Fig. 3.8).

## Prusik Knot

Although technically a hitch, the prusik is usually referred to by climbers as a knot. The prusik has a variety of applications, but it is commonly used to attach a rope of smaller diameter (5–7mm) to one of a larger diameter (9–11mm) for the purpose of ascending or anchoring a rope. When properly tied, the prusik has the ability to grip the larger diameter rope when tension is placed on it, but will slide easily along the rope when tension is released (Fig. 3.9).

Knot tying is an important skill, as it plays a significant role in climbing safety. Knots for climbing should be practiced until they are known by heart!

## Runners

Runners (also referred to as slings) are most commonly constructed of one-inch nylon webbing, 5 ft long (Fig. 3.10). A water knot is used to tie the two ends together. Longer runners can be constructed of one-inch nylon webbing, 10 ft long. Many climbers are now using runners in which the ends have been sewn together to form a loop. Although runners that have been sewn together are stronger

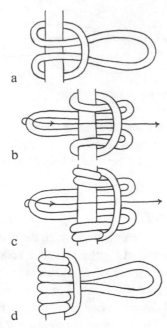

**Figure 3.9a-d** The prusik knot.

than tied runners, climbers should make a habit of checking each sewn runner before use to ensure that the stitching is intact. When in doubt, retire the runner.

## Construction of Climbing Harnesses

There are several ways that a harness may be constructed. Although a swami belt, consisting of several wraps around the waist with 1–2 in. webbing, is the easiest to construct, it is not recommended unless used in conjunction with leg loops. A swami belt used by itself may cause internal organ damage or broken ribs should the climber experience a hard fall or be forced to hang for a long period of time.

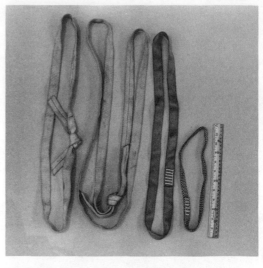

**Figure 3.10** Examples of runners with the ends tied together and runners with the ends sewn together

A harness with leg loops that provides safety as well as comfort can be constructed by following the steps listed below. A minimum of 20–25 ft of one-inch webbing is required.

1. The webbing is first doubled in half with a small overhand knot tied in the end. A second overhand knot is tied in *one* of the tails approximately 4–5 in. from the first (Fig. 3.11a).

2. Both tails are passed between the legs keeping the two overhand loops in front. Each tail is then brought around the front of each corresponding leg and passed through the overhand loop (Fig. 3.11b).

3. The leg loops are pulled snug with the longer of the two tails passed around the back to the opposite hip. It is at this juncture that a square knot is snugly tied to hold up the leg loops (Fig. 3.11c).

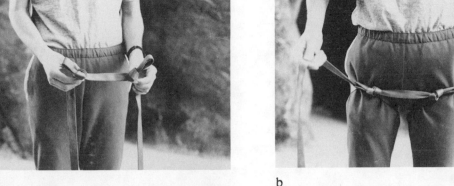

a

b

c

d

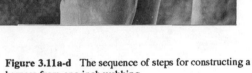

**Figure 3.11a-d** The sequence of steps for constructing a harness from one-inch webbing.

4. The remaining webbing is wrapped in opposite directions around the waist. The two free ends of webbing should be secured with a water knot (Fig. 3.11d). A climbing rope can then be attached to both the bottom loop and through all of the waist loops. When using this type of harness, it is important to periodically check all knots to be sure they are still tied.

—John R. Kascenska, II—

17

# MOVEMENT ON ROCK IV

## General Guidelines

The fear of falling is a legitimate response to a precipitous position on high angle rock. Fear is known by all climbers, and it must be dealt with, lest one become paralyzed in a precarious position and suffer serious consequences. One overcomes fear by practicing in an environment in which a fall will have no serious consequences. This is insured by the use of a climbing rope and specialized hardware, and the necessary skills and good judgment to use both correctly. These skills will be dealt with in later chapters.

There are a number of principles that hold in rock climbing. One important principle is that the climber should try to keep his weight over his feet as much as possible. One can comfortably walk up a steeply angled slab if one's weight is over one's feet. However, as soon as the weight is shifted forward, the feet tend to slip. Although rock climbing shoes with sticky soles will greatly enhance the climber's ability to ascend high angle slabs, the climber must maintain an upright posture.

A mistake that beginners often make is to become "spread-eagle" on a rock. From this position, any movement will usually result in a fall. Rather, the climber should try to keep his body in alignment as much as possible. One's position when climbing a vertical wall should resemble as closely as possible that of a person climbing a ladder. Arms and legs should not be extremely off-center. Thus, if a hand or foot should slip, the body won't be thrown to one side causing a fall.

The "ladder" model illustrates another important concept. The climber should climb with his feet, and only on the more extreme climbs should he use his arms for anything more than balance. For security against unexpected falls, the climber should move from a base support of two feet and one hand or, minimally, from a position of two hands and one foot. In extreme positions, as mentioned earlier, the climber must use either one or two arms to pull himself up the rock without help from his legs. This technique requires considerable upper body strength and may be used only intermittently with rest stops in between.

Famed mountaineer, Paul Petzoldt, always advised beginners to "climb with your eyes". The climber should plan the route ahead as far as is possible from the ground. The proposed line should be carefully scrutinized for each usable foothold and handhold. Rest stops should be utilized to further study the route lying above the climber. Not only should the route be studied for its ascent potential, but consideration should be given in case the climber may have to down-climb. Additionally, a route should be analyzed for potential hazards in case a fall is sustained, and the climber must be rescued by either the partner or by the climber, himself.

19

Practitioners of Zen disciplines such as judo and karate often note similarities between their style and that of a particular animal. Though not practicing a Zen discipline, rock climbers would do well to emulate the movements of the cat. A cat will briefly pause at the base of a tree before its first leap to a stable position. From there it will move smoothly and without hesitation to a rest position. There it will pause and rest until its next uninterrupted move to a higher position. Beginning climbers, unlike the cat, will not study the route and usually pounce on the rock like a squirrel intent on a mad dash to the summit. Soon, legs begin to tremble as the upper body clings to the rock and fingertips quickly tire, sending the body back to earth with an inglorious crash. From the cat there is much to learn.

When climbing where a fall would have no consequence, i.e., a top-roped situation, the beginner should always push himself until he either has to down-climb or falls. All too often, the beginning climber will climb to a point where he runs into difficulty, and, instead of pushing himself to the limit, he acquiesces and drops voluntarily. If a line has been picked that completely dead-ends, the climber should attempt to down-climb the route. Both pushing your limits and utilizing techniques of "down-climbing" will enhance overall climbing ability.

## Body Position

Even though body position has been mentioned relative to one's weight over the feet, a more detailed discussion is necessary. Body position changes relative to the terrain. A climber must alter position constantly depending upon whether he is negotiating a steep slab, a vertical or slightly overhanging wall, or

Figure 4.1 Upright body position on near-vertical wall.

a chimney. Steep slabs, as mentioned earlier, are negotiated with the weight directly over the feet. The climber is in an upright to slightly crouching position, using the hands only for balance. Movement must be slow and weight transfers done smoothly.

When the terrain shifts to vertical or near vertical, the body must be held out from the wall, as the climber must be able to see both foot and handholds (Fig. 4.1). A common mistake is for the beginner to grab for a handhold, and then blindly churn with both feet. Instead, the climber must lean out far enough to see potential foot placements. The foot should be carefully placed on the best available foothold and the weight then transferred to that foot. Either a smooth transfer or a gentle hop off of the opposite foot should follow.

a                                                                b

**Figure 4.2a-b** Sequence of moves in climbing chimney.

On slightly overhanging walls, the climber shifts his hips slightly into the wall and leans his upper body away from the wall in order to keep his weight directly over his feet. He will be able to see farther ahead by utilizing this technique. When the wall actually juts out horizontally, or nearly so, as under an overhang, the climber reaches as high as possible with his hands, then brings his feet as high as possible under the overhang, pulls or pushes with the palms or fingers, and finally brings his feet up over the overhang.

## Chimneys

Chimneys (cracks wider than 10 in.) represent a unique formation that require the use of counter-force to climb. The back is usually pressed against one wall, and the hands extend to the opposite side securely lodging the climber in the crack. Upward progress is made by bringing the legs up with the feet on opposite sides of the wall. The legs straighten 1– 2 ft as the arms relax, and, then the climber locks the upper body again, starting the inchworm maneuver all over again (Fig. 4.2). The real challenge comes when the chimney flares, and the climber must rest both hands on one side and both feet on the opposite side of the chimney. Progress here becomes strenuous.

The opposite extreme is when chimneys narrow down into cracks. Cracks that may be climbed range in size from those large enough for the insertion of an arm and possibly a leg to those just large enough to insert the fingers up

**Figure 4.3** Toe jams.

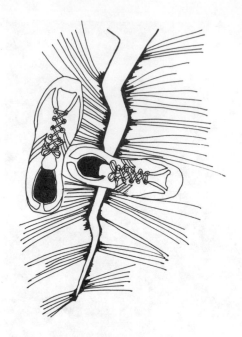

**Figure 4.4** Stacked feet in a squeeze crack.

to the first joint. Foot and hand placement play an important part in crack climbing.

## Foot Placement

Careful and deliberate foot placement is the cornerstone of a good climber's arsenal. If the climber's vertical ascent is not to be limited by the number of chin-ups he can do in combination with bomb-proof handholds, then he must learn to use his feet effectively.

A foothold may be either a sharp edge, a smooth depression, or a crack. The inside edge of the shoe is used to mount sharp edges. The toe is generally less stable on small edges. More rounded depressions are better used by placing the ball of the foot in the depression, and twisting or "smearing" the sole of the shoe into the hole. Generally the heel should be allowed to drop to a level even with the ball

of the foot; otherwise, fatigue quickly sets in followed by a case of "sewing machine leg".

The toes may be placed in cracks as narrow as 1 1/2 in. by twisting the foot outward with the knee orientated toward the outside and torqueing the toe by pulling the knee toward the crack (Fig. 4.3). Slightly larger cracks may be jammed with the entire foot utilizing a similar technique. Even larger cracks may be climbed by stacking both feet (Fig. 4.4).

## Handholds

Handholds generally assist in balance and are rather infrequently used as in a gymnastic high bar event. Thus, very small nubbins and edges often suffice which would be inadequate if the entire weight of the body had to be supported. The entire weight of the body may only

Figure 4.5 Ring grip.

Figure 4.6 Pinch grip.

Figure 4.7 Thumb and fingers exerting counter-pressure.

occasionally be supported by both or only one handhold.

The most obvious handhold is an edge over which the fingers are cupped. A noteworthy point is that the thumb is the strongest of all the fingers. Thus, a ring grip with the thumb and index finger locked together over an edge is much stronger than the index and three smaller fingers alone (Fig. 4.5). Other formations lend themselves to pinch grips (Fig. 4.6).

The combination of various widths and shapes of cracks and the adaptability of the fingers and hand create an endless number of variations (Fig. 4.7–4.9). From an insertion of one joint of the pinky finger to a full fist jam, the variations of handholds in cracks are only limited by imagination. Climbers not only use handholds to pull upward, they use them to pull downward. Figure 4.10 illustrates the use of counter-force to stabilize the climber. This maneuver is known as a lie-back.

A mantel is a move involving a push downward with one or both hands and is used in mounting a shelf. A mantel can be a strenuous move at the end of an overhang. The foot is the last body part to be brought up to hand level (Fig. 4.6).

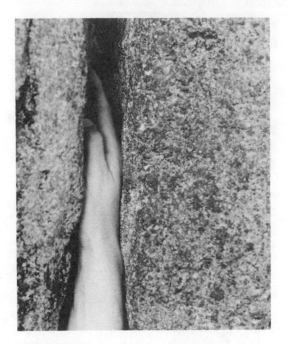

**Figure 4.8**  Hand jam.

**Figure 4.10**  Lie-back.

**Figure 4.9**  Fist jam.

**Figure 4.11**  Mantel Sequence.

—Horace T. Bone—

24

# BELAYING

# V

## Introduction

The word "belay" is a nautical term meaning to secure a rope. Rock climbers have adopted the term to mean the securing of the rope between climber and "belayer" in case of a fall by the climber. Mountaineering history is rife with examples of entire roped parties being pulled off of a mountain by the fall of a single climber. In the celebrated Whymper expedition of 1865, three men were pulled off the face of the Matterhorn by the fall of a fourth.

These early alpinists climbed on fairly steep snow and ice, all moving simultaneously. In the event of a fall, all members of the rope team would go into a self-arrest position with their ice axes, hoping to jointly stop the fall of the leader or fallen member. This method usually worked except on very steep ice or snow.

A rock climber, however, has no chance of stopping his falling partner unless he is securely anchored and able to apply friction to the rope going to the fallen climber. Belaying is this entire technique of anchoring oneself and then bringing a falling climber to a stop by either snubbing the rope around one's own body or running it through a friction device.

## Anchors

Anchoring oneself is the first prerequisite to a successful belay. Indeed, the belayer *must*

**Figure 5.1** Ground belay position.

be secured in a stable position relative to any forces which may result from the attached falling climber. If the belayer is thrown forwards, backwards or even sideways, the least effect will be a loss of concentration and a likely ineffective belay. The anchor for a ground belay need only protect against a force that will lift the belayer off the ground in the case of a fall (Fig. 5.1).

Multi-pitch climbs of more than one rope length call for anchors that protect the belayer against both upward and downward forces. There is always a possibility that the climber may fall past the belayer, and the belayer may be violently pulled in a downward direction. Assuming an effective placement of protection, however, the force of the falling climber will pull the belayer upward. Therefore, the belayer is obliged to place either a failsafe multidirectional anchor that will resist a force from any direction, or a combination of unidirectional anchors that when tied together resist both upward and downward forces (Fig. 5.2). The optimal combination of unidirectional anchors would be two anchors to protect against a downward pull and one anchor to protect against an upward pull.

If only one or two unidirectional anchors are placed to protect against a downward pull, they should be placed as high as possible. In the event, then, of an upward pull, the force would not likely be great enough to pull the belayer above the level of his anchor(s).

## Belay Systems

There are two methods that the belayer may use to apply friction to the rope in order to stop a fall. The first method uses the belayer's own body as a "snubbing post" and is commonly known as the sitting or standing hip belay. A second method uses any of several mechanical devices to apply friction to the rope. The hip belay should be learned before the mechanical methods for several reasons. The hip belay requires the least amount of equipment. The hand movements are identical with those used in mechanical systems, and the frictional forces generated are quite satisfactory for top-roping. The hip belay, however, is not recommended for the belay of a lead climber. The force generated by a falling lead climber will likely cause the rope to be ripped through the belayer's hands, and, at most, the

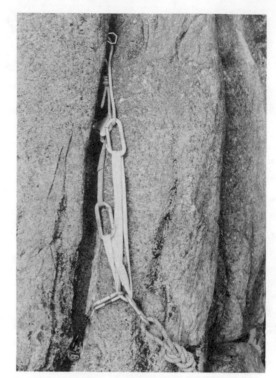

**Figure 5.2** Combination of two anchors to protect against a downward pull and one anchor to protect against an upward pull.

falling climber will be slowed only slightly before either hitting the ground, a ledge or the end of the rope.

### The Hip Belay

The hip belay requires that the rope from the climber be passed around the belayer's waist and be held securely by the brake hand. The belayer may be either seated or standing. In the event of a fall, the belayer moves his brake hand in a direction to increase the friction of the rope running around his body. Padding around the waist and a leather glove increase the effectiveness of the hip belay.

The movement of the hands is critical to a proper hip belay. Figure 5.3 illustrates the proper movement of the brake and non-brake

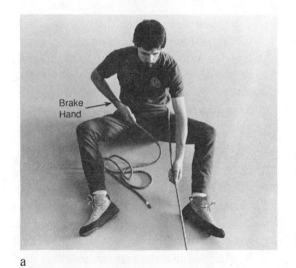

Brake
Hand

a

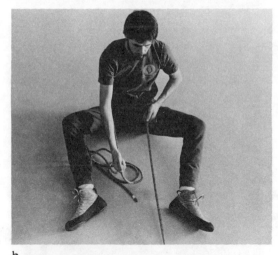

b

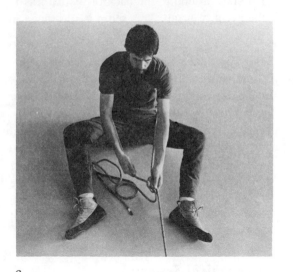

c

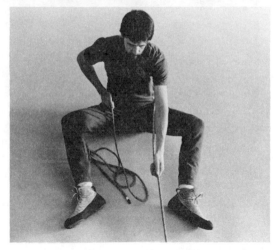

d

**Figure 5.3a-d** The hip belay—rope retrieval sequence.

hand when taking in rope. The beginning belayer should practice these movements along with the movement of the brake hand until the proper use of the hands becomes an almost reflex action. A moment's hesitation or an incorrect movement of the brake hand could prove fatal in a real situation. The most common mistake in the movement of the brake hand occurs when the non-brake hand grasps both strands of rope *below* the brake hand. This necessitates letting go of the rope with the brake hand in order to get a new purchase when retrieving rope. The non-brake hand should only grasp both strands of rope *above* the brake hand. This is a mistake made by many experienced climbers. It may be fatal!

**Figure 5.4** Standing hip belay. Note carabiner placed at waist to prevent rope being pulled up back or below knees.

Letting rope out is straightforward. Move one hand at a time. Never allow the brake hand to leave the rope and be prepared to brake at all times.

A further point should be noted when setting up a hip belay. Care should be taken that the rope running around the waist will not be pulled up the back or down to the knees in the event of a fall. If this were to happen, the belayer would find himself holding the rope in one hand without the frictional advantage of the rope running around his waist. This may be avoided by one of two methods. If in a given situation the only possible force would be to pull the rope upward, then the belayer should run the rope from the climber *under* the anchor and to the brake hand. If the only possible force would be to pull the rope downward, then the belayer should run the rope from the climber *above* the anchor and to the brake hand.

A belayer who is not at ground-level, however, may experience either an upward or downward pull on the rope in the case of a fall. To avoid the rope being pulled either up the back or down to the knees, the rope from the climber should be run through a carabiner that is then clipped into the harness, so that it cannot slide around to the back of the harness in the event of a fall. This setup is illustrated in figure 5.4.

The final point in setting up a hip belay deals with rotational forces on the belayer. If the brake hand is on the same side as the tether that attaches the belayer to his anchor, the belayer will experience a strong rotational force in the event of a fall. If the brake hand and tether are on opposite sides, the belayer will experience no rotational force, as the force from the tether and the climbing rope will negate each other, the forces being equal and opposite.

## Mechanical Systems

A mechanical belay system may be attached to the belayer's harness, or it may be attached directly to an anchor. Direct attachment to an anchor is preferable if the anchor is "bombproof". The belayer will not experience the force of the falling climber, and the belayer may exit the system more easily if he is not directly involved in the system. If the anchor is suspect, however, as in the case of a bolt(s), the attachment should be to the belayer's harness. This minimizes forces on

a

b

**Figure 5.5a-b** The Munter Hitch.

the anchor, as the belayer's body must first be moved by the force of the falling climber before any force is transmitted to the anchor.

The recommended mechanical belay system is the Munter Hitch (Fig. 5.5). A locking pear-shaped carabiner designed for use with the Munter Hitch should be used, and, as stated previously, may be clipped into the front of the harness or directly to the anchor. The belayer may or may not be attached to the same anchor depending upon its security. The movement of the hands is similar to the movement of the hands with the hip belay. In the case of a fall, the brake hand should hold the rope securely, the hitch will lock on the carabiner, and the falling climber will be brought to a smooth stop due to the dynamic properties of the modern climbing rope.

Two other mechanical systems are the Figure-8 descender and the Sticht plate. The Figure-8 descender may be used in a top-rope situation (Fig. 5.6), though it should never be used to belay a leader as illustrated. The friction generated will be insufficient to stop a fall of any distance. The Figure-8 descender may be used to belay a leader if used as a Sticht

**Figure 5.6** The Figure-8 descender belay.

plate. A bight of rope is first passed through the small hole and clipped through a locking carabiner (Fig. 5.7). The Sticht plate (Fig. 5.8) is commonly used, though it has a major disadvantage. The brake hand must be moved into the correct position after the fall in order to cause the rope to lock against the plate. This disadvantage applies equally to a Figure-8 descender used as a Sticht plate. It is also possible to inadvertently lock the rope. This can cause a lot of stress if the climber happens to be on a delicate move.

**Figure 5.7** The Figure-8 descendcer used as a Sticht plate.

**Figure 5.8** The Sticht Plate belay. Note "keeper" cord.

## Additional Notes on Belaying the Leader

An examination of the physics of falling bodies yields some startling facts. A 150 lb climber who leads 10 ft above a midpoint belayer and then falls can generate a force on his body in excess of 3000 lbs. He will have fallen a total of 20 ft, and the entire force will have been dissipated over only 10 ft of rope. If, however, the climber had climbed 40 ft

above the belayer without placing a running belay before falling, he would have fallen a total of 80 ft and would have generated approximately 1,350 lbs force. The force relayed to the fallen climbers's body is indirectly related to the amount of rope stretch. Therefore, the length of a fall is less important than the length of rope between the belayer and climber, i.e., the more rope length, the less severe the force on the climber's body. This also holds for the force transmitted to the belayer.

If the climber who climbed 10 ft and fell had placed a running belay 5 ft above his belayer and clipped into it, he would have fallen only 10 ft, generating significantly less force. The force on the belayer would have been upward—a much easier force to hold. Additionally, the force on the belay anchor will be less if the belayer puts himself into the system rather than belaying directly to the anchor, as the belayer's body must be lifted before any force can come onto the anchor.

Though the force generated on the falling climber's body is directly related to the length of the fall and indirectly, to the length of rope extended, the force transmitted to the belayer is additionally related to the number of intermediate belay points. The force at the belayer is less than that from the climber by the amount of frictional resistance generated as the rope binds over the carabiner at each belay point, i.e., the more the number of intermediate belay points, the less the force on the belayer in the case of a fall. Climbers have no reluctance to place protection before a difficult move, but often neglect placing adequate protection early in the lead. The protection of the belayer and his anchor through early placement of running belays is more important than the placement of protection high on the climb.

# Signals

A set of signals should be agreed upon that is simple and leaves little possibility for confusion. The following set is suggested and is in common use.

**ON BELAY**—Belayer to climber. Indicates that belayer is ready and will remain so until climber is safely anchored. May be posed as a question by the climber.

**CLIMBING**—Climber to belayer, in response to ON BELAY.

**CLIMB**—Belayer to climber, meaning to go ahead.

**UP ROPE**—Climber to belayer. Indicates there is slack in the rope. Please take it up.

**SLACK**—Climber to belayer. Indicates that the climber needs a few feet of slack rope. Belayer gives only a few feet. If necessary, climber will ask for additional slack.

**TENSION**—Climber to belayer. Indicates that the belayer should pull hard on the rope. Sometimes needed in order to make a difficult move or when removing a piece of protection.

**ROCK!**—*Always* used by climber when *any* object dislodged or dropped.

**FALLING**—Might as well give your belayer all the advance warning possible.

**BELAY OFF**—Climber to belayer. Indicates that the belayer may end his duty to the climber and begin his own preparation to climb. Note the difference in sound between ON BELAY and BELAY OFF. This convention should be followed in order not to have the two signals confused. OFF BELAY should not be used, as it sounds similar to ON BELAY.

**THANK YOU**—Not said to be polite by either party. Indicates that one has heard the previous communication but may not be able to immediately follow up with the usual action. An example of the use of THANK YOU is when a climber reaches a belay ledge and sets up an anchor. The climber then yells ON BELAY. The partner, however, is still involved in removing his own anchor and cannot climb immediately. Thus, he answers THANK YOU. The partner knows he has been heard and can cease screaming ON BELAY!

—Horace T. Bone—

# PLACEMENT OF PROTECTION

VI

## Introduction

Both the belayer and the climber must be anchored to the wall by the placement of either natural or artificial anchors. The belayer should be anchored securely by the placement of at least two solid anchors. The climber places running belays along his route and clips the climbing rope to them by means of a carabiner. Running belays prevent the climber from falling to the ground or past his belayer if they are placed at appropriate points.

The beginning climber should learn the art of placement through a diligent study of appropriate publications and by studying the placement of a competent leader. Manufacturers of climbing gear publish detailed descriptions of appropriate use of their gear, as they have a libelous interest in the proper use of their products. The improper use and placement of protective devices is worse than no protection at all, as poorly placed protection only gives a false sense of security.

## Natural Anchors

Though they are used interchangeably, belays are considered either "natural" or "artificial". Natural belays involve the slinging of a tree, tunnel, rock projection, chockstone, or expanded flake with a carabiner clipped onto the sling (Fig. 6.1).

**Figure 6.1** A natural rock projection "slung" for protection. Note climbing rope clipped through a carabiner that is attached to the sling.

Particular care should be taken that rope drag does not lift a runner from a horn or flake. The runner may be tied securely around the horn with an overhand knot, or it might be weighted with equipment. Runners should be arranged so that a fall will not cause them to be flicked off. As always, the climber must be keenly aware of potential forces if he falls, and how they will affect his protection.

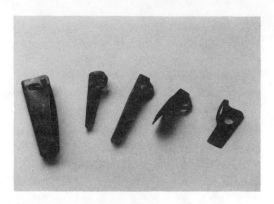

**Figure 6.2** Assorted pitons.

## Artificial Anchors

### Pitons

Artificial anchors involve the use of pitons, chocks, camming devices, and wedging devices. Each type of protection can be only briefly mentioned, though the climber should make a thorough study of each type before using them.

Pitons were originally soft iron wedges that were driven into cracks with a hammer. A carabiner was then clipped through a hole in the piton. These pitons conformed to the crack and were left in place for subsequent climbers. A hundred or more of these pitons had to be carried to protect a climb of any severity. In 1947, John Salathe forged a set of hard steel pitons out of the axle of a Model-T Ford and used them on the first ascent of Lost Arrow Spire in the Yosemite Valley. He found these pitons had superior holding power, and they could be removed and reused. Today pitons are manufactured from chrome molybdenum alloy and are available in a number of shapes (Fig. 6.2).

Pitons are generally not used today because they scar rock, and other forms of protection are usually available that work as well. However, in the case of an incipient crack that can be protected in no other way, the use of a piton would be justified. Also, on first ascents of unknown difficulty, or on remote walls where a fall could be serious, pitons are occasionally used. Pitons should not be used on popular routes in major climbing areas.

### Chocks

The British were the first to utilize natural chockstones for protection. A rock lodged in a crack made an excellent point of protection provided the crack tapered downward to resist movement of the rock. It wasn't long before climbers started carrying a pocketful of pebbles to place in appropriately sized cracks to sling for protection. The next step was to carry several sizes of machine nuts with a sling tied through the hole. These could be placed in cracks and a carabiner clipped through the sling for protection.

Today chocks are cast or machined into three basic shapes—hexcentric, wedge, or asymmetrical. Hexcentrics, like wedges and asymmetricals, come in a series of graduated sizes and are slung with either rope, sling or cable (Fig. 6.3).

Hexcentric or wedge shaped chocks must be placed in cracks that narrow and cause the chock to resist a downward pull. Because the climbing rope can often lift chocks, a runner is usually placed between the chock and the climbing rope.

The most useful asymmetrical chock is the Tricam—a piece that locks itself in a crack because of its three-point camming action. Note that the sling *must* be properly oriented to cause the cams to operate properly (Fig. 6.4).

**Figure 6.3** Chocks. Left to right—Tricam, Hexcentric, slung Stopper, wired Stopper.

**Figure 6.5** Friend placed in a crack.

**Figure 6.4** Tricam showing proper orientation of sling.

## Friends

In 1978, Ray Jardine invented the Friend—a device with four spring-loaded ec- centric cams that directed the load of a fall toward the walls of a crack (Fig. 6.5). Friends finally enabled the climber to utilize vertical flaring cracks for protection. Recently, Flexible Friends and similar designs have been added to the climbers' repertoire. They utilize a flexible cable instead of a solid shaft to load the axle of the cams. The 1988 "Wild Country" catalog offers the following suggestions for the placement of Friends:

- Always align stem, and thus cams, to the direction of loading.

- Don't offset cams—they have little holding power. Realign the cams evenly.

- Avoid wide open placements of cam tips.

- Always use a sling long enough to ensure you won't move a unit by climbing past it.

- Don't allow the cams to invert—inverted cams won't hold.
- Don't stuff a "too large" unit into a small spot, it may make removal difficult.
- Bottoming cracks should be avoided as they make cleaning difficult, and they may hinder any stem alignment in a fall. (Even though flexible units will work in such positions, stems aligned in the direction of loading are always more secure.)
- Never place a rigid stem so that it cannot align to the direction of the load.
- Always regard flexible stems as less predictable than rigid stems.

## Wedging Devices

Several companies are manufacturing devices that employ a stacking or wedging theme (Fig. 6.6). Rock 'n Rollers (Go Pro, Inc.) incorporate a cylinder on a wedge. Sliders (Metolius Mountain Products) and Quickies (D. Best Mountaineering) consist of two metal wedges attached to wires. These wedging devices work best in thin parallel-sided cracks, but tend to pop out of flaring cracks.

## Some Guidelines for the Placement of Protection

A basic concern in the placement of protection is alignment. If all running belays are placed in a straight vertical line, a fall will place a downward pull on the closest carabiner. Force will not come on lower belay points unless the upper piece pulls out. In practice, however, belay points are seldom placed in vertical alignment. Thus, a fall will transmit forces along the entire string of running belays that may be diagonal or even upward. Direc-

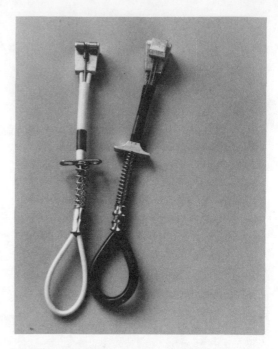

**Figure 6.6** Wedging devices. Left to right—Rock'n Roller, Quickie.

tional belays may be pulled out. If the top anchor pulls, the entire system may collapse (Fig. 6.7).

An alignment of the system may be effected by the use of runners (Fig. 6.8). Additionally, the first piece of protection is often placed to take an upward or sideways pull in the case of a fall. This will tend to keep the forces parallel to the rope if the belayer is located out from the wall.

For further guidance in the placement of protection, excellent descriptions are to be found in Royal Robbin's *Advanced Rockcraft* (La Siesta Press, Glendale, CA, 1985), Michael Loughman's *Learning to Rock Climb* (Sierra Club Books, San Francisco, CA, 1981), and *Mountaineering: The Freedom of the Hills* (The Mountaineers, Seattle, WA, 1982).

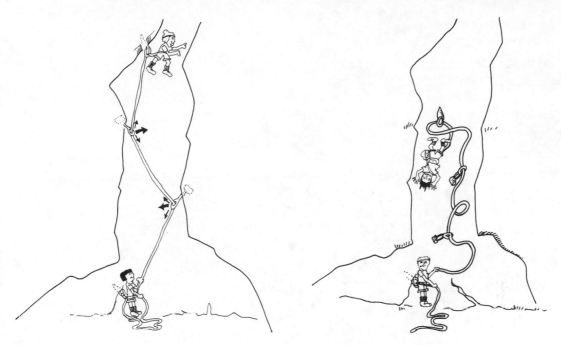

**Figure 6.7** Arrows indicate direction of forces during a fall. Entire system may fail during a fall.

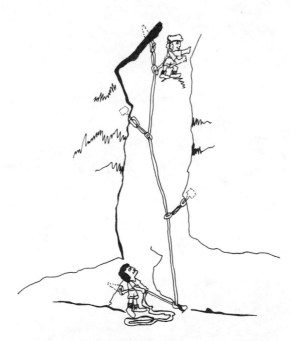

**Figure 6.8** Proper alignment using runners and an initial chock set to take an upward force.

—Horace T. Bone—

37

## Introduction

Few skills excite the inexperienced climber more than rappelling—the act of descending a fixed rope. Experienced climbers, though, avoid rappelling whenever possible. The act of sliding down the rope is relatively simple and can be learned in an afternoon. The associated skills of route selection, anchor placement, throwing the rope, and retrieval of the system are critical, and a single mistake may bring down the entire system.

## Anchoring the System

Rappel anchors are even more critical than belay anchors, because the entire weight of the climber and his equipment will come on the rappel anchor for an extended period of time. Generally, one solid anchor will suffice if it is either a solid boulder, a solid rock projection, or a live tree at least 4 in. in diameter. Boulders or rock projections should be inspected for fracture lines, crumbly surfaces or sharp edges. The attachment of a tree to the rock should be noted. Do the roots spread out over the surface of the rock, or do they grow solidly into a crack system? The direction of force against the anchor should be considered. Will the pull tend to stabilize or destabilize the anchor? If fixed pitons, bolts or chocks are used, at least two or possibly three anchor points should be utilized. Bolts and bolt

**Figure 7.1** Rappel rope through sling.

hangers are always suspect. Never rappel off one bolt.

Tubular or flat webbing, or rope may be used to sling anchors. Though flat webbing does not roll as easily as rope, it cuts easily when loaded. Therefore, either pad or round off any sharp edges that may cut the sling. The angle where the rappel rope passes through the sling should be no greater than 60 degrees (Fig. 7.1), and it should be away from the rock if possible. The length of the sling may be adjusted to effect the correct angle and cause the

a

b

**Figure 7.2a-b** Correct adjustment (a) and incorrect adjustment of sling (b) to alleviate friction on a rappel rope.

rope to be away from the wall where it passes over the sling (Fig. 7.2). Significant friction may otherwise develop at this point and make rope retrieval extremely difficult.

Multiple anchor points should be connected by a common sling so that equal tension is applied to each anchor. This is often referred to as a self-equalizing anchor system. The rappel rope should not be run over the sling but rigged as in figure 7.3, where the

**Figure 7.3** A single twist placed in one strand of a sling so that the failure of one anchor will not cause the carabiner (or similiarly placed rappel rope) to slide off the sling.

failure of one anchor will not cause the rappel rope to slip off the sling.

Bolts at rappel points are often joined by a short section of chain. The rappel rope should not be run over the chain where failure of the chain would cause the rope to slide off of the chain. Again, the bolts should be joined by a short section of sling as described above, and the chain may be disregarded as it is an unnecessary link that may be bypassed by a stronger piece of sling webbing.

On popular climbs, one will find dozens of slings left behind by previous parties. These slings are always suspect. Ultraviolet radiation, time and exposure to the weather all contribute to the loss of strength of nylon. The sheen is lost and slings become dull when exposed for any length of time. If previously left slings are used, use no less than two of them. Inspect them for abrasion, check the knots and rotate them enough to place the strain and abrasion at different points.

Many experienced climbers opt for a belay whenever practical. This practice is highly recommended if the first climber is unsure of himself, if the rappel may end at an overhang, or the belay anchor is less than optimal. If the need is related to the uncertainty of the rappel anchor, a second anchor should be established to anchor the belayer. The second person down would remove the belay anchor and usually rappel with a self-belay.

## Route Selection

The ideal rappel route should be nearly vertical, directly above the exit point and featureless except for appropriate belay points. Sharp edges in particular should be avoided. As the rappel rope repeatedly elongates and then contracts under the weight of the climber, it may rub against a sharp edge and be severed. Debris-covered ledges also constitute a hazard, as the rope may dislodge rocks that either hit the climber or sever the rappel rope at a lower point. While descending a rock-strewn gully in the Wind Rivers one evening, I dislodged a rock that started a minor rock avalanche beneath me. Only the next day did I discover that my rappel rope had been nearly severed by a rock. Vertical cracks should be avoided, because the rope may lodge in a crack when being retrieved. Overhangs constitute another hazard, as the climber will have to ascend his rope unless he can reach the wall and a belay point.

Guide books usually note the location of rappel points and assume that the climbers have two ropes of 165 ft length each. These rappels are usually the best choice particularly if they are marked with slings left by previous climbers. You may not be able to locate these points, however, and should, therefore, note appropriate ledges and other advantageous points as you ascend.

In spite of having noted belay ledges on the ascent and having solemnly memorized the guide book description of the location of the rappel point, one may still become lost and, even if not lost, have darkness descend upon one's party. This will not be a time for sudden haste. Sit down, take note of your situation and decide if it is better to bivouac or continue in darkness. There are no rules, but there are rational and irrational decisions, dependent upon the circumstances. The first rational decision would have been adequate preparation for a possibly cold, wet bivouac.

## Throwing the Rope

In the case of a rappel of less than one-half the rope length, the rope may be run through the belay sling to the midpoint of the rope and each half then thrown separately. Each half to be thrown is divided equally and coiled in the two hands. The half closest to the midpoint is thrown first and, then, the second half is thrown. The process is repeated for the other half of the rappel rope. If either half of the rappel rope tangles and does not run cleanly down the wall, it must be retrieved and thrown again. *A Figure-8 knot should be tied into the end of each half.* This will prevent the climber from falling off the end of the rope if a mechanical rappel system is being used.

If the rappel is over one-half the length of a climbing rope, two climbing ropes should be tied together with a Figure-8 follow-through knot, provided they are of equal diameter. Ropes of unequal diameter should be tied together with a Double Fisherman's knot. Ropes of unequal diameter may stretch unequally when loaded and may compensate by sliding around the belay sling and cut it. Ropes of different construction type (kernmantel and laid) should definitely not be used in combination, as they exhibit significant differences in elongation. No problem is usually noted, however, if both ropes are of similar construction and no greater difference in diameter than 3 mm. The knot should be placed so that it will not have to ride around the belay sling when one of the ropes is pulled to retrieve the system. The rope that is to be pulled should also be placed under the other rope, as pulling the upper rope could cause the lower rope to bind. If the ropes are otherwise indistinguishable, the rope to be pulled should have a double knot placed in its end to distinguish it.

## The Body Rappel

The body rappel (Fig. 7.4) is a technique that utilizes the friction of the rope running over the body to slow the descent. The technique is simple; it utilizes a minimum of equipment and is fairly comfortable on slopes of moderate angle. It is, however, uncomfortable at a steeper angle or over overhangs unless some padding is provided for the shoulder and crotch area.

To get into the body rappel, stand facing the anchor and straddle the rope. With the left hand, reach between the legs, grasp the rope and pull it in front. Lift the rope over the head and across the *opposite* shoulder. Reach back with the left hand and grasp the rope. The left hand will be the control or brake hand—the one that will control the rate of descent. The right hand will be used only for balance. Of course, the entire setup could be reversed with the right hand being the control hand.

If the anchor is set high enough, it will be possible to take up all slack in the rope and ease over the wall in a standing position. If the

**Figure 7.4** The body rappel.

anchor point is below the waist, it will be easier to start in a sitting position with the legs dangling over the wall and the right shoulder facing outward. With all slack removed from the system, lock the brake hand and rotate the body counter-clockwise toward the anchor. This will cause you to slip over the wall, and the body will be supported by the system. Push out with the feet against the wall until the body is at an angle of about 60 degrees from the wall and the feet about shoulder width apart. Let the rope slide through the brake hand to descend the rope.

Descend at a smooth steady pace. *Do not jump*! This places a tremendous load on the anchor as the body rapidly decelerates. It may, also, seriously abrade or cut the rope at a sharp edge if it repeatedly elongates and then returns to its original length with each bound of the

**Figure 7.5** Figure-8 descender rappel.

climber. Forget all the movies and the Army commercials that picture high-speed bounding rappels down cliffs. They aren't rappelling off of 1/4 in bolts.

## The Figure-8 Descender Rappel

The Figure-8 descender rappel is a highly recommended mechanical system. Though it does require a piece of specialized equipment, it is simple, reasonably fast to set up, and almost failsafe with reasonable precaution. The climber should wear a commercial or tied harness with this technique.

First, face the anchor and make a bight with both strands of the rappel rope. While holding the descender with the large hole upward or toward the anchor, force the bight through the large hole and bring it around the neck above the small hole. Then, clip the small hole into a locking carabiner clipped to the harness (Fig. 7.5), so that the force comes on to the leg loops, not the waist band. Take the rope in the right hand which will be the brake hand. Of course, either hand may be utilized as the brake hand.

There will be sufficient friction on the rope to easily stop the descent with the brake hand. The left hand should act as a guide hand above the descender. If additional friction is required, the brake hand may be brought around the back of the waist. The hands may be freed altogether by wrapping the rope in several figure-of-8's around both thighs or single wraps around one leg. The retrieval of the rappel ropes will be eased significantly if they are not allowed to twist together.

Some climbers will not carry a Figure-8 descender, because it has a singular use. They prefer to rig a 6-carabiner brake rappel system because it utilizes common items always carried on fifth class climbs. I rappel on almost every climb. I prefer to have the simplest most failsafe mechanical system available for an activity fraught with so many potential hazards.

## The Carabiner Brake Rappel

Having just disparaged the carabiner brake rappel, I must now backup. A climber *should be able* to rig a carabiner brake rappel. It does use items of equipment always carried on fifth class climbs. It may be used in the absence of specialized gear, and the system does have variations commonly used in rescue situations. I have, in the past, given my Figure-8 to a less experienced climbing partner, and reverted to the carabiner brake rappel for myself.

The carabiner brake rappel is complicated, though there is little chance it will malfunction if rigged correctly. The correct sequence is to clip a locking carabiner into the harness so that the body weight will be on the leg loops. Two carabiners may be used in the place of a locking carabiner if the gates are opposed as shown

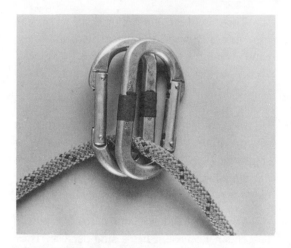

**Figure 7.6** Carabiners with gates opposed.

**Figure 7.7** Carabiner brake rappel.

in figure 7.6. Clip two more carabiners into the original locking carabiner with their gates opposed. These two carabiners will lie in a vertical plane. Stand facing the anchor and take a bight of the doubled rope and force it through the second pair of carabiners. Clip two additional carabiners across the second pair of carabiners *so that the bight will bind against the spines of the last pair of carabiners.* If the last pair of carabiners is placed with the gates facing the bight, the bight will open the carabiners when weight comes onto the rappel rope. See figure 7.7 for an example of the completed system.

The rope may be held in either hand off to one side at arms's length. To increase friction, the brake hand may be moved around the back of the waist. If more friction is desired, the rope may be passed completely around the waist and held in the opposite hand. Hair and loose clothing can easily be caught in the braking system. Therefore, tuck in loose items of clothing and tuck long hair into the shirt.

The descent should be slow and smooth, with the non-brake hand being held above the carabiners for balance. A rapid descent may cause the carabiners to heat up enough to burn the hand or the rope at the end of the descent.

## Retrieving the Rappel Rope

The ease with which the rappel rope may be retrieved is usually related to skill in selection of the route and placement of the anchor. If friction has been reduced by the proper placement of the belay sling, and the route chosen has few cracks and ledges, then, the rope will likely be easy to retrieve.

Check to see that the ropes are not twisted together and be certain to pull the rope with the knot under the sling. The rope to pull should have been identified by a distinctive knot if not otherwise distinguishable. Pull with a slow steady speed. Avoid jerking the rope. This may cause it to lodge in a crack or around a projection. If the rope will not move, try pulling from a different direction. If feasible, get farther away from the wall. This will further reduce friction, and make it less likely for the ropes to bind together.

If the rope will fall below you, make sure it is tied to an anchor. More than one climber has had to suffer the indignity of explaining how he lost his rope when it fell past him and was jerked out of his hand. Alternatively, it may be threaded through the second belay sling by one party member as the first member pulls the rope.

If all goes well, the rope will come careening down the wall and either fall at your feet without associated rocks or will sail past you and lie straight as an arrow below you. This does not always happen. As often as not, the rope will sail past you in a series of loops and land on ledges, in the tops of trees and may even knock off a climber below you if you haven't been considerate in your selection of a rappel route. The same considerations apply when pulling the rope up to you as when pulling it down. Pull slowly and steadily. Consider changing position. Try snaking loops down the rope to flip it out of a crack or a tree branch. Pray!

## When the Rope Hangs Up . . .

Notice the use of the declarative, "When the rope hangs up" as opposed to the subjunctive, "If the rope hangs up." Sooner or later, every climber is faced with a hung rope. What to do? I suggest these cognitive steps:

1. Take a 5 minute break.

2. Consider and try anything you might not have tried to free the rope.

3. If you have enough spare rope and equipment, consider a lead climb to the point where the rope is hung up.

4. Anchor the belay rope. Rig a self-belay and ascend the hung rope while simultaneously placing protection alongside the rope.

5. Yell loudly, "HELP", at timed intervals. When no one comes, prepare to spend the evening.

6. Begin yelling, "HELP", at regular intervals beginning at daybreak. Continue until the onset of laryngitis.

7. Consider the ascent of the hung rope without the benefit of protection. (Highly recommended for the terminally ill and those of hypocerebral function.)

## The Self-Belay

As previously mentioned, a climber on rappel will often request a belay from his partner if he is either insecure about his personal skill or the security of the anchor. An alternative is the self-belay or Prusik belay. The Prusik belay is fashioned by tying a loop of 5–7 mm rope onto the rappel rope above the brake with a Prusik knot and tying or clipping the loop to the harness with a locking carabiner (Fig. 7.8). The Prusik loop should always be a smaller diameter than the climbing rope (a 7 mm loop will not work well with a 8.5 mm climbing rope). The loop should attach to the rappel rope approximately 2 ft above the harness and always within reach of the rappeller.

As you descend, slide the Prusik knot along the rappel rope with your non-brake hand. If the Prusik knot is released, it will jam tightly against the rope, stopping your descent. Once jammed, the knot can only be released if weight can be taken off of it. This can be accomplished by tying a second Prusik loop onto the rappel rope and standing in it to take weight off the first knot. Always carry a second loop.

**Figure 7.8** Carabiner brake rappel with Prusik loop self-belay.

**Figure 7.9** Position of prusik loops to ascend a fixed rope. Note tie-in to fixed rope.

Many young bold climbers disdain either a belay from a partner or a self-belay. Suffice it to say that there are many young bold climbers. There are few old bold climbers. A partner belay will protect against failure of the anchor, failure of the rappel rope, falling out of the brake system, and may save your life if you are hit on the head by a rock. A self-belay will not protect against failure of the anchor or the rappel rope.

## Ascending

The Prusik knot is not only used as a self-belay, it can, also, be used to ascend a rope. This may become a necessity if the climber falls while attempting an overhang and cannot reach the wall. It may, also, become a neces-

sity if the climber rappels beyond an overhang, and the rope does not reach the ground or a belay point.

Two slings of approximately 6 1/2 ft length and 5–7 mm diameter are required to ascend a fixed rope. One of the slings is shortened by tying a figure-8 on a bight in the center of the sling. This sling is then attached to the fixed rope with a Prusik knot. A carabiner is clipped above the figure-8 knot and then clipped to the harness. The second sling is attached to the rope below the shortened sling. Either one or both feet are placed in this sling (Fig. 7.9).

To ascend, stand up in the lower sling with both feet and slide the upper harness sling higher. Then transfer the weight to the harness sling. Again, stand up in the lower sling, loosen the Prusik knot and slide the upper harness sling higher. To decrease the likelihood of a severe fall if the upper sling should fail, the climber should attach the rope below the lower sling to his harness with a locking carabiner. An ever lengthening loop of rope will hang below the climber as he ascends. This rope should periodically be untied and retied just below the lower sling to decrease the length of a fall if the upper sling should fail.

The Prusik ascent should be practiced before it becomes a necessity. It is easy to become confused and attach the slings in the wrong position on the rope. At best, the climber will only be delayed 10 or 15 minutes until he deciphers the system. At worst, he could accidentally release himself and fall.

—Horace T. Bone—

# RATING OF CLIMBS

## Introduction

Rating systems give the rock climber an idea of the difficulty to be expected on a climb. Ratings are usually assigned by an experienced climber along with the consensus of those climbers who repeat the route. The level of difficulty is generally based upon such criteria as number and size of handholds/footholds, steepness of the cliff, exposure and length of the climb. The level of difficulty is also based upon the hardest free move or section encountered on a particular route. For example, a climb given a rating of 5.9 (see below) may only have one short section of difficulty while the remainder may be quite easy. Finally, it is important to recognize that rating systems are subjective. They are, however, useful as a guide in choosing routes that match the skill level of the climber, in addition to measuring a climber's skill development. Below are explanations of the classes, decimal system, grades and aid climbing ratings as they apply to rock climbs in the United States.

## The Classes

The rating system most commonly used throughout the United States was first based upon a system of classes introduced by the Sierra Club in the 1930's. This rating system consists of six classes and is described as follows:

Class 1—Walking or hiking over varied terrain.

Class 2—Scrambling up steep slopes with occasional use of the hands for balance.

Class 3—Climbing with some use of the hands. A rope may be needed for the inexperienced climber where there is moderate exposure.

Class 4—Climbing where the hands are definitely needed for balance. Most climbers will want a rope due to the increase in exposure. Climbers are usually belayed.

Class 5—Climbing where protection is placed by the leader. Ropes and hardware are not used as a means of ascending.

Class 6—Aid climbing. The climber actually places his weight upon the rope and anchors as a means of ascending.

## The Decimal System

During the 1950's, climbers at Tahquitz Rock in California found the need to further delineate climbs that fell into the class 5 rating. A decimal point plus a numerical rating of 0–9 were added to the class 5 distinction, thus creating the Decimal System. Climbing routes with a rating of 5.0 were considered to be the easiest, while those assigned a rating of

5.9 were considered to be the most difficult class 5 climbs at that time.

Problems with the decimal system eventually developed. This was due to the closed-end nature of the decimal rating system and the ascent of routes of increasing difficulty. However, the mathematical significance of the decimal point was eventually ignored and the rating scale was extended to include 5.10 (or five–ten). Over the years increasingly difficult climbs have been accomplished to the point where the climbing scale now ranges from 5.0 to 5.14. In addition, the range of difficulty for those climbs on the upper end of the scale (5.10–5.14) are further differentiated by the letters a, b, c, and d. For example, a 5.10a is less difficult than a 5.10d. As a guide for the beginner, climbs with ratings of 5.0 to 5.3 may be considered easy; 5.4–5.6, moderate; 5.7–5.9, difficult; and 5.10–5.14, extremely difficult.

## The Grading System

A grading system was also introduced in the 1950's to describe the overall time commitment required by experienced climbers to ascend a particular route. Factors that determine this commitment involve both objective dangers and overall physical strain. More specifically, these factors include length of the climb, number of difficult pitches, routefinding problems, and stonefall. This system consists of grade I through grade VI and can be used in conjunction with the decimal system (example: Grade III, 5.7). It should be recognized that these grades only apply when climbing conditions are optimal. Listed below is the approximate amount of time commitment associated with each grade.

Grade I—May take a few hours.

Grade II—May take up to a half day.

Grade III—Almost a full day.

Grade IV—1–1.5 days.

Grade V—1.5–2 days.

Grade VI—2 or more days.

## Aid Climbing Ratings

The aid climbing rating system was designed to describe a portion(s) of a climbing route that requires the climber to use aid techniques to complete an ascent. More specifically, the aid climbing rating system describes the adequacy of the protection that supports the climber's weight as well as the difficulty of placement. The rating of aid climbs consists of A0 through A5 and is used in conjunction with the decimal system (example: 5.11, A2).

A0—Fixed anchor.

A1—Solid anchor placements.

A2—Awkward for the climber to place but solid.

A3—Anchors can hold short falls.

A4—Anchors can hold only the body weight.

A5—Thirty or more feet of continuous A4.

## Other Rating Systems

Although no attempt will be made to describe them, it should be mentioned that other rating systems do exist, and the climber may on occasion come across them. Examples include the Australian system, British system and the National Climbing Classification System (NCCS).

# ETHICS FOR ROCK CLIMBING AND THE ENVIRONMENT

## Introduction

In virtually all outdoor activities in which increasing numbers of individuals participate, some evidence of human use will be left behind. Popular rock climbing areas are no exception. Many climbing areas are showing significant signs of wear and tear. Although damage to the rock itself has diminished over the years due to the use of climbing protection that leaves no scars when removed, other environmental impacts are evident. Some environmental impacts that are evident include damaged and cut trees, litter, excessive erosion of primary and secondary trails leading to climbing sites, deposition of human feces, the presence of old fire rings, and overused campsites.

It is true that some environmental impacts are the result of careless practices by other visitors and not just climbers. Regardless of who may be at fault, it is important that all users of the outdoors respect and protect the environment they utilize. Many of this Nation's natural areas are under a policy of "regulation by numbers." This policy exists in part because of the environmental damage the area has suffered. Some climbing areas are also regulated, mostly due to safety considerations, but also for environmental reasons.

## Ethics for Rock Climbing

Rock climbers have a responsibility to ensure that climbing routes are not altered or defaced in any manner. This includes refraining from altering the rock to create or eliminate handholds. In addition, the use of removable chocks and other camming devices will leave the rock in good condition. Although pitons were used extensively in the past, the age of clean climbing has virtually ruled out their placement. Pitons found on established routes, however, should be left in place. Although there is still much debate regarding the use of bolts, it is commonly agreed upon that bolts should not be added to existing routes. Bolts found on established routes, however, should be left in place.

## Ethics for the Environment

Climbers not only have a responsibility to help preserve the condition of the rock by using clean climbing methods, but to also help preserve the surrounding environment. Environmentally minded climbers can help reduce the degree of impact created by doing their part. This includes staying on designated trails to the cliff area to prevent the establishment of secondary trails and the erosion that will follow. Secondary trails usually occur as a result of people who short-cut designated trails that snake their way to the base of a cliff.

Vegetation encountered should also be left intact so those who follow may enjoy the naturalness of the cliff and surrounding areas. In addition, all litter and food items should be packed out.

There are several minimal impact camping techniques that can be practiced by climbers who decide to camp (if camping is permitted) within the vicinity of the cliff site. First, campers should use stoves instead of fires for cooking. The use of stoves will help conserve wood supplies in addition to reducing the effects of poor fire building practices. Poor fire building practices include fires built on top of organic ground layers or against reflecting rocks. Heat from a fire built on top of an organic ground layer has the capability of altering organic matter to a depth of four inches, adversely affecting regrowth of vegetation. Fires built against reflecting rocks cause permanent blackening and unnatural exfoliation.

Second, pots and pans used in cooking should be washed away from water sources, not in them. Waste water should be poured into a "sump hole" dug into the organic ground layer.

Third, great care should be taken in choosing a tent site. Hampton and Cole (1988) suggest several criteria for choosing a tent site. Tent sites should be located on level dry areas to minimize the effects of soil compaction, soil erosion and the effect on vegetation. Campsites should also be located well away from water sources, trails and beauty spots. Visual impact can be minimized in forested areas, but the ecological impact to soils and vegetation are clearly less in meadows and resilient grassy areas. Hampton and Cole also suggest that campers should use either high-impact campsites or pristine campsites. High-impact campsites are popular locations where most of the ground vegetation has been lost due to trampling. This type of campsite is preferred, as further use will cause little additional deterioration. Pristine campsites are locations that show no signs of previous use, and should *only* be used if a high-impact site is not available. Key practices that can be implemented if staying in a pristine site include taking time to find the most resilient site (dry grass, sand, bedrock, or snow), staying only one night, and keeping party sizes to a small number. Campsites that show signs of previous use, but have a substantial amount of vegetation still surviving, are generally referred to as low—or moderately-impacted. This type of campsite should be avoided, as the site will deteriorate with further use but will eventually recover if unused.

Fourth, solid human waste and toilet paper should be disposed of properly, preferably in an established latrine facility (if available). If a latrine facility is not available, human feces should be buried in a cathole dug into the organic ground layer well away from water sources and other campsites. If toilet paper is used, it should either be burned and buried or packed out.

Finally, campers should do the best they can to camouflage the campsite area, disguising the fact that they have camped by spreading leaf litter and replacing rocks and logs that may have been temporarily set aside. More in-depth information on minimal impact techniques can be found in Bruce Hampton and David Cole's *Soft Paths* (Stackpole Books, Harrisburg, PA. 1988).

This last chapter is one the authors felt was necessary. Our country is now approaching the state where our natural resources are precious and few. Therefore, it is the responsibility of all outdoor recreationists to be good stewards of the land and treat it with respect, so those that follow may enjoy the environmental qualities found to be special. It is also the responsibility of rock climbers to help educate those individuals less experienced and knowledgeable of the ethical rock climbing and environmental practices discussed above.

—John R. Kascenska, II—

# REFERENCES

Hampton, B. and Cole, D., **Soft Paths**, Harrisburg, PA: Stackpole Books, 1988.

Loughman, M., **Learning To Rock Climb**, San Francisco, CA: Sierra Club Books, 1981.

March, B., **Modern Rope Techniques In Mountaineering**, 2nd ed. Worsley, Manchester, England: Cicerone Press, 1976.

Mendenhall, R. and Mendenhall, J., **The Challenge of Rock And Mountain Climbing**, Harrisburg, PA: Stackpole Books, 1976.

Peters, E., ed. **Mountaineering: The Freedom Of The Hills**, 4th ed. Seattle, WA: The Mountaineers, 1982.

Robbins, R., **Advanced Rockcraft**, Glendale, CA: La Siesta Press, 1985.

Setnicka, T.J., **Wilderness Search And Rescue**, Boston, MA: Appalachian Mountain Club, 1980.

Wheelock, W., **Ropes, Knots And Slings For Climbers**, Glendale, CA: LA Siesta Press, 1982.

Wilson, K., ed., **The Games Climbers Play**, San Francisco, CA: Sierra Club Books, 1980.

# GLOSSARY

**Aid Climbing**—The method by which a climber ascends a route by using ropes and hardware to support his weight.

**Arete**—A sharp outward facing corner formation on a cliff.

**Belay**—A method by which an individual (belayer) manages the rope in such a way as to anchor the rope should the climber fall.

**Bolt**—A form of protection or intermediate anchor that consists of an expansion bolt driven into a previously drilled hole in the rock.

**Bowline**—A knot used to construct a non-slipping loop. It can also be used to attach a climbing rope to a harness or a rope around a climber's waist.

**Bouldering**—A variety of climbing where a person may traverse or ascend a particular route without a rope for protection, but usually climbs only a few feet off the ground with a spotter.

**Buttress**—An outward facing corner on a cliff, generally much broader than an arete.

**Carabiner**—A snaplink made of aluminum alloys or steel and commonly used to link together rope, webbing, or other carabiners.

**Chimney**—A feature in a rock cliff that will accept a climber's body.

**Chocks**—Artificial pieces of climbing protection of varying shapes and sizes that serve as an anchor when wedged into a crack in the rock.

**Class**—Any one of six divisions (Class 1–6) to describe the type of terrain expected on a route from hiking to aid climbing.

**Crux**—The most difficult move or section of a particular climbing route.

**Decimal System**—A numerical grading system (5.0 to 5.14) that gives the climber an idea of the difficulty to be expected on a climbing route.

**Dihedral (Open Book)**—An inward facing corner of a rock cliff that resembles the inside corner of a wall.

**Double Bowline**—A knot used to construct a non-slipping loop. It can also be used to attach a climbing rope to a harness or a rope around a climber's waist.

**Double Fisherman's Knot**—A knot used to join two ends of climbing rope of the same or dissimilar diameters.

**Figure-8 Descender**—An aluminum alloy device that when attached to a rope will allow a climber to rappel down a rope or belay a climber.

**Flemish Bend**—A synonym for figure-8 follow-through knot.

**Friend**—An artificial piece of climbing protection consisting of four movable cams that allow the device to be placed in a wide range of cracks.

**Grade**—Any one of six divisions (Grade I–VI) that describes the time commitment required by the climber to complete an ascent.

**Harness**—A web-like belt system worn by the climber to which the climbing rope is attached. Climbing harnesses support the climber and distribute the forces generated by a fall.

**Hexcentric**—A six-sided piece of aluminum alloy that when wedged in a crack provides an anchor for the climber.

**Jam Crack**—A crack that varies in width from hand size to leg size.

**Jumar**—A device that when attached to a suspended climbing rope allows the climber to ascend the rope. The device will freely travel over the rope as it is moved upward, but will lock in place when weight is placed upon it.

**Kernmantel Rope**—Refers to the construction of a specific type of climbing rope. This type of construction consists of a nylon core (kern) under a braided, protective sheath (mantel).

**Laid Rope**—Refers to the construction of a specific type of climbing rope. This type of construction consists of small nylon fibers twisted into a larger strand. Three of these larger strands are then wound tightly together.

**Lead Climbing**—A type of climbing in which a climber with rope attached to a harness will climb a route, periodically placing intermediate anchors as he ascends. The person who is the first to ascend a route is considered the lead climber.

**Lie-back**—A climbing technique by which a climber ascends a highly angled crack by placing both hands in the crack with feet close to the hands. The climber stays on the rock by pulling outward with the hands while keeping the feet against the rock.

**Mantel**—A technique by which a person climbs over a shelf-like rock feature by placing hands on the shelf, pushing downward with the arms, and stepping onto the shelf with the feet, all in a sequential manner.

**Munter Hitch**—A friction hitch that is used for belaying.

**Overhand Knot**—A knot commonly used in climbing as a "safety knot" to prevent more complex knots from coming untied.

**Overhang**—A section of a cliff that exceeds a 90 degree angle.

**Pendulum**—A term used to describe the wide arching fall taken by a climber who climbs too far to the right or left of the fall line of the rope.

**Pitch**—A term used to describe the distance or rope length between belay stances or points on a particular route. A climbing route may be several "pitches" in length.

**Piton**—An artificial piece of protection consisting of a metal blade of chrome molybdenum alloy that can be hammered into a crack in the rock. At one end of the blade is a hole to which a carabiner can be attached.

**Protection**—A term used to describe natural and artificial anchors used by climbers to secure the rope and themselves to the rock face.

**Prusik Knot**—A knot used to secure a rope of smaller diameter (5–7mm) to a rope of larger diameter (9–11mm) for the means of ascending or anchoring a rope.

**Ramp**—A wide ledge tilted at an angle.

**Ring Bend**—A synonym for water knot.

**Roof (Ceiling)**—A feature in a cliff that resembles a wall that is perpendicular to or overhangs a vertical cliff face.

**Runner (Sling)**—A short piece of webbing or rope tied together to form a loop.

**Second**—The next person after the lead climber to ascend a particular climbing route.

**Smearing**—A climbing technique whereby the bottom portion of the climbing shoe is pressed or "smeared" against the rock surface to gain maximal friction.

**Sticht Plate (Belay Plate)**—A device used as a mechanical belay to help anchor the rope in the event a climber should fall.

**Stemming**—A climbing technique by which a climber may ascend a chimney or dihedral by pressing against the sides with the feet.

**Stopper**—A wedge-shaped nut or piece of aluminum alloy which is attached to a piece of wire cable, sling or rope.

**Swami Belt**—A climbing harness formed by making a series of wraps around the waist with 1–2 inch nylon webbing and securing the ends with a water knot.

**Top-roped Climbing**—A variety of climbing where the climber is protected by a rope anchored from above. The climber is tied into the rope with one end, while a second climber serves as the belayer and manages the other end.

**Rappel**—A technique by which a climber lowers himself down the side of a cliff using the rope.

**Figure-8 Follow Through Knot**—A knot commonly used to attach a climbing rope to a harness.

**Water Knot**—A knot used to attach two ends of nylon webbing.